MW00511298

PLANT BASED DIET COOKBOOK FOR BEGINNERS

50 Recipes to Indulge in Mouthwatering Plant-Based Treats

By Lisa Oliveri

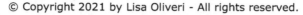

© Copyright 2021 by Lisa Oliveri - All rights reserved.

The following Book is reproduced below with the goal of providing information that is as accurate and reliable as possible. Regardless, purchasing this Book can be seen as consent to the fact that both the publisher and the author of this book are in no way experts on the topics discussed within and that any recommendations or suggestions that are made herein are for entertainment purposes only. Professionals should be consulted as needed prior to undertaking any of the action endorsed herein.

This declaration is deemed fair and valid by both the American Bar Association and the Committee of Publishers Association and is legally binding throughout the United States.

Furthermore, the transmission, duplication, or reproduction of any of the following work including specific information will be considered an illegal act irrespective of if it is done electronically or in print. This extends to creating a secondary or tertiary copy of the work or a recorded copy and is only allowed with the express written consent from the Publisher. All additional right reserved.

The information in the following pages is broadly considered a truthful and accurate account of facts and as such, any inattention, use, or misuse of the information in question by the reader will render any resulting actions solely under their purview. There are no scenarios in which the publisher or the original author of this work can be in any fashion deemed liable for any hardship or damages that may befall them after undertaking information described herein.

Additionally, the information in the following pages is intended only for informational purposes and should thus be thought of as universal. As befitting its nature, it is presented without assurance regarding its prolonged validity or interim quality. Trademarks that are mentioned are done without written consent and can in no way be considered an endorsement from the trademark holder.

Table of Contents

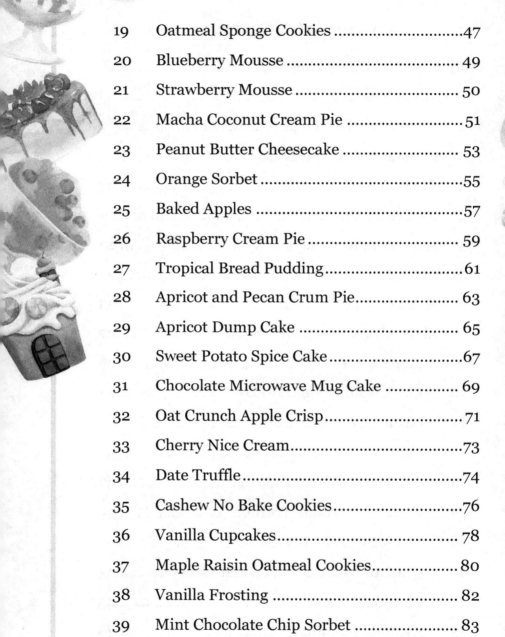

Plant Base Diet Guide Line

It is a natural fact that only through watching what we eat will we have the most impact on our weight. Plant-based diet really helps you and let you appreciate automatic, easy fat burning without all the usual calorie constraints of other diets.

Weight loss is an almost certain result you will enjoy once you start the plant-based diet, but this is not the only benefit that you will enjoy. Think of all those activities you have always wanted to pursue but shelved because you simply had no energy left after your usual day's work.

Well, it's time to dust off those hobbies and the things you enjoy doing, because on the plant-based you will have more energy for your daily work and play! The accompanying mental clarity and sharpness of thought are also positive effects which you will have as a direct result of the diet. A better health report card, by way of optimized cholesterol readings, normalized blood sugar and a corresponding lowered risk of cardiovascular diseases are also just some of the beneficial health effects experienced by most on the diet.

This book's aim is primarily to give you the tools with which to let the diet run more smoothly and seamlessly in your daily life. Something that many learn is that a diet is almost only as good as the number of recipes it has in its repertoire. The benefits of a particular diet may be numerous, but if you are forced to have the same stuff every breakfast, lunch and dinner, even the most avid supporter would probably have problems sustaining the diet. This is where I am most happy to say that the plant-based diet has quite some leeway for the concoction of various different recipes, and it is the purpose of this book to bring you some of the more delicious and easy-to-prepare meals for your gastronomic pleasure!

For the beginners as well as the adepts, the recipes contained within are created specifically to be appealing to your palate, while not requiring you to literally spend the whole day in the kitchen! Concise and to the point, the recipes break down meal preparation requirements in a simple step-by-step format, easy for anyone to understand.

Over the past 5 years, scientific articles have shown the substantial benefits of increasing your consumption of plant-based foods. Studies show that adopting a more

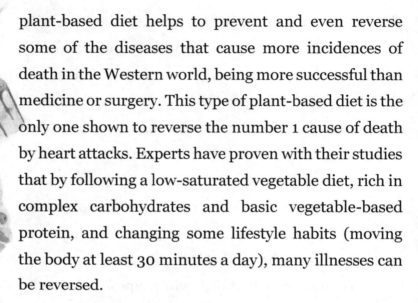

plant-based diet helps to prevent and even reverse some of the diseases that cause more incidences of death in the Western world, being more successful than medicine or surgery. This type of plant-based diet is the only one shown to reverse the number 1 cause of death by heart attacks. Experts have proven with their studies that by following a low-saturated vegetable diet, rich in complex carbohydrates and basic vegetable-based protein, and changing some lifestyle habits (moving the body at least 30 minutes a day), many illnesses can be reversed.

A vegetable-based diet also helps prevent certain types of cancer, reduces the incidences of heart disease and diabetes, Cholesterolemia, Hypertension, Alzheimer's, Parkinson's Disease, Rheumatoid Arthritis, Ulcers, and Vaginal Infections.

A plant-centered diet has a positive effect on the prevention of accumulation of abdominal fat, the appearance of acne, aging, allergies, asthma, body odor, cellulite, eczema, Metabolic Syndrome, and body weight control.

We can not only increase the chances of improving our life expectancy by increasing our intake of fruits and vegetables, but also ensure a life with a higher quality of health. However, the consumption of meat and other foods of animal origin, including dairy products, have shown that (possibly due to its high content of saturated fats, arachidonic acid, and hemo metal), life expectancy is shortened.

Consumption of meat, fruit, milk, and eggs often increases exposure to toxins, mercury and other heavy metals and xenoestrogens that are produced when fish is cooked at high temperatures, and carcinogenic substances in meat.

Contrary to popular belief, in their diet, most Vegans do get enough protein, consume more nutrients than the average omnivore, and typically maintain a more appropriate weight. There are only 2 vitamins that we can't find in plant foods; these are vitamin D, that we get from exposure to the sun, and vitamin B12, produced by micro bacteria that live on the earth, and from which one should be supplemented.

Desserts Recipes

1 Brown Rice Pudding

Preparation Time: 15 Minutes

Cooking Time: 1 Hour 15 Minutes

Servings: 2

Ingredients:

- ½ cup brown basmati rice, soaked for 15 minutes and drained
- 1½ cups water
- 2½ cups unsweetened almond milk
- 4 tablespoons cashews
- 2–3 tablespoons maple syrup
- 1/8 teaspoon ground cardamom
- Pinch of salt
- 3 tablespoons golden raisins
- 2 tablespoons cashews
- 2 tablespoons almonds

Directions:

1. In a pan, add the rice and water over medium-high heat and bring to a boil.
2. Lower the heat to medium and cook for about 30 minutes.
3. Meanwhile, in a blender, add the almond milk and cashews and pulse until smooth.

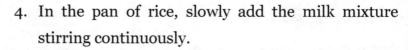

4. In the pan of rice, slowly add the milk mixture stirring continuously.

5. Sir in the maple syrup, cardamom, and salt, and cook for about 15–20 minutes, stirring occasionally.

6. Stir in the raisins and cook for about 15–20 minutes, stirring occasionally.

7. Remove from the heat and set aside to cool slightly.

8. Serve warm with the garnishing of banana slices and pistachios.

Nutrition: Calories: 498; Protein: 11g; Carbohydrates: 73g; Fats: 21g

2 Cinnamon Coconut Chips

Preparation Time: 10 Minutes

Cooking Time: 25 Minutes

Servings: 2

Ingredients:

- ¼ cup coconut chips, unsweetened
- ¼ teaspoon of sea salt
- ¼ cup cinnamon

Directions:

1. Add cinnamon and salt in a mixing bowl and set aside. Heat a pan over medium heat for 2 minutes.
2. Place the coconut chips in the hot pan and stir until coconut chips crisp and lightly brown.
3. Toss toasted coconut chips with cinnamon and salt.
4. Serve and enjoy!

Nutrition: Calories: 228; Fats: 21g; Carbohydrates: 8g; Protein: 2g

3 Peach Cobbler

Preparation Time: 20 Minutes

Cooking Time: 4 Hours

Servings: 4

Ingredients:

- 4 cups peaches, peeled and sliced
- ¼ cup of coconut sugar
- ½ teaspoon cinnamon powder
- 1 ½ cups vegan sweet crackers, crushed
- ¼ cup stevia
- ¼ teaspoon nutmeg, ground
- ½ cup almond milk
- One teaspoon vanilla extract

Directions:

1. In a bowl, mix peaches with coconut sugar and cinnamon and stir.
2. In a separate bowl, mix crackers with stevia, nutmeg, almond milk, and vanilla extract and stir.
3. Shower your slow cooker with cooking spray and spread peaches on the bottom.
4. Add crackers mix, spread, cover, and cook on Low for 4 hours.
5. Divide cobbler between plates and serve.

Nutrition: Calories: 212; Fat: 4g; Carbohydrates: 7g; Protein: 3g

4 Ice Cream

Preparation Time: 10 Minutes

Cooking Time: 4 Hours to freeze

Servings: 5

Ingredients:

- 1 ½ teaspoon of natural vanilla extract
- 1/8 teaspoon of salt
- 1/3 cup of erythritol
- 2 cups of artificial coconut milk, full fat

Directions:

1. Stir together the vanilla extract, salt, sweetener, and milk.
2. If you do not come up with an ice cream machine, freeze the mixture in ice cube trays, then use a high-speed blender to blend the frozen cubes or thaw them enough to meld in a regular blender or food processor.
3. If you have an ice cream machine, just blend according to the manufacturer's directions.
4. Eat as it is or freeze for a firmer texture.

Nutrition: Calories: 184; Protein: 2g; Carbohydrates: 4g; Fat: 19g

5 Almond Butter Fudge

Preparation Time: 15 Minutes

Cooking Time: 3 Hours to freeze

Servings: 8

Ingredients:

- 2 ½ tablespoons coconut oil
- 2 ½ tablespoons honey
- ½ cup almond butter

Directions:

1. In a saucepan, pour almond butter then add coconut oil warm for 2 minutes or until melted.
2. Add honey and stir.
3. Pour the mixture into a candy container and store it in the fridge until set.
4. Serve and enjoy!

Nutrition: Calories: 63; Fat: 5g; Carbohydrates: 6g; Protein: 0.2g

6 Chocolate with Coconut and Raisins

Preparation Time: 10 Minutes + chilling

Cooking Time: 0 Minutes

Servings: 20

Ingredients:

- 1/2 cup cacao butter, melted
- 1/3 cup peanut butter
- 1/4 cup agave syrup
- A pinch of grated nutmeg
- A pinch of coarse salt
- 1/2 teaspoon vanilla extract
- 1 cup dried coconut, shredded
- 6 ounces dark chocolate, chopped
- 3 ounces raisins

Directions:

1. Combine well all the ingredients, except for the chocolate, in a mixing bowl.
2. Spoon the mixture into molds. Leave to set hard in a cool place.
3. Melt the dark chocolate in your microwave. Pour in the melted chocolate until the fillings are covered. Leave to set hard in a cool place.

4. Enjoy!

Nutrition: Calories: 130; Fat: 9g; Carbohydrates: 12g; Protein: 1g

7 Mocha Fudge

Preparation Time: 15 Minutes + 1 Hour Freezing

Cooking Time: 0 Minutes

Servings: 20

Ingredients:

- 1 cup cookies, crushed
- 1/2 cup almond butter
- 1/4 cup agave nectar
- 6 ounces dark chocolate, broken into chunks
- 1 teaspoon instant coffee
- A pinch of grated nutmeg
- A pinch of salt

Directions:

1. Line a large baking sheet using a parchment paper.
2. Melt the chocolate in your microwave and add in the remaining ingredients; stir to combine well.
3. Scrape the batter into a parchment-lined baking sheet. Place it in your freezer for at least 1 hour to set.
4. Cut into squares and serve. Bon appétit!

Nutrition: Calories: 105; Fat: 6g; Carbohydrates: 13g; Protein: 1g

8 Almond and Chocolate Chip Bars

Preparation Time: 10 Minutes + 30 Minutes Freezing

Cooking Time: 0 Minutes

Servings: 10

Ingredients:

- 1/2 cup almond butter
- 1/4 cup coconut oil, melted
- 1/4 cup agave syrup
- 1 teaspoon vanilla extract
- 1/4 teaspoon sea salt
- 1/4 teaspoon grated nutmeg
- 1/2 teaspoon ground cinnamon
- 2 cups almond flour
- 1/4 cup flaxseed meal
- 1 cup vegan chocolate, cut into chunks
- 1 1/3 cups almonds, ground
- 2 tablespoons cacao powder
- 1/4 cup agave syrup

Directions:

1. In a mixing bowl, thoroughly combine the almond butter, coconut oil, 1/4 cup of agave syrup, vanilla, salt, nutmeg, and cinnamon.

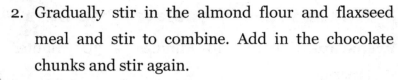

2. Gradually stir in the almond flour and flaxseed meal and stir to combine. Add in the chocolate chunks and stir again.

3. In a small mixing bowl, put and combine the almonds, cacao powder, and agave syrup. Now, spread the ganache onto the cake. Freeze for about 30 minutes, cut into bars and serve well chilled. Enjoy!

1. **Nutrition:** Calories: 295; Fat: 17g; Protein: 2g; Carbohydrates: 35g

9 Almond Butter Cookies

Preparation Time: 30 Minutes

Cooking Time: 15 Minutes

Servings: 20

Ingredients:

- 3/4 cup all-purpose flour
- 1/2 teaspoon baking soda
- 1/4 teaspoon kosher salt
- 1 flax egg
- 1/4 cup coconut oil
- 2 tablespoons almond milk
- 1/2 cup brown sugar
- 1/2 cup almond butter
- 1/2 teaspoon ground cinnamon
- 1/2 teaspoon vanilla

Directions:

1. In a mixing bowl, put and combine the flour, baking soda, and salt.
2. In another bowl, combine the flax egg, coconut oil, almond milk, sugar, almond butter, cinnamon, and vanilla. Put the wet mixture into the dry ingredients then stir until well combined.

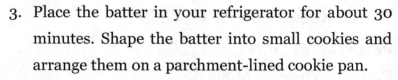

3. Place the batter in your refrigerator for about 30 minutes. Shape the batter into small cookies and arrange them on a parchment-lined cookie pan.

4. Bake in the preheated oven at 350 degrees F for approximately 12 minutes. Moved the pan to a wire rack to cool at room temperature. Bon appétit!

Nutrition: Calories: 197; Fat: 15g Carbohydrates: 12g; Protein: 2g

10 Black Bean Orange Mousse

Preparation Time: 5 Minutes

Cooking Time: 15 Minutes

Servings: 6

Ingredients:

- 4 tbsp. Cashew Milk
- 15 oz. Black beans
- Zest of 1 Orange
- 1.7 oz. Dates, pitted
- 5 tbsp. Cacao Powder, raw
- 2 tbsp. Coconut oil, melted
- 8 tbsp. Brown Rice Syrup

Directions:

1. First, place the black beans and dates in the food processor.
2. Process them for 2 to 3 minutes or until finely grated.
3. Next, add all the remaining ingredients to the food processor and process it again.
4. Finally transfer the mixture to the serving bowls and sprinkle it with cacao nibs.

Nutrition: Calories: 486; Total fat: 8g; Carbohydrates: 82g; Protein: 22g

11 Cashew Pudding

Preparation Time: 10 Minutes

Cooking Time: 25 Minutes

Servings: 2

Ingredients:

- ¼ cup Cocoa Powder, unsweetened
- 1 cup Cashews, raw
- Dash of Sea Salt
- 4 tbsp. Almond Milk, unsweetened
- 2 Medjool Dates
- 1 tbsp. Maple Syrup
- 1 tbsp. Coconut Oil

Directions:

- First, place the cashews in a medium bowl along with hot water. Soak it for one hour.
- Next, transfer the soaked cashews into a high-speed blender along with the remaining ingredients.
- Blend for 2 minutes or until you get a smooth and creamy mixture.
- Now, return the pudding to the bowl and cover it with a plastic wrap.
- Finally, keep the bowl in the refrigerator for 2 to 3 hours or until set.

- Serve and enjoy.

Nutrition: Calories: 459; Protein: 14g; Carbohydrates: 49g; Fats: 28g

12 Vanilla Mug Cake

Preparation Time: 1 Minutes

Cooking Time: 4 Minutes

Servings: 1

Ingredients:

- ¼ cup Cashew Milk
- 1 scoop Vanilla Protein Powder
- ¼ tsp. Vanilla Extract
- 1 tsp. Chocolate Chips
- ½ tsp. Baking Powder
- 1 tbsp. Granulated Sweetener of your choice
- 1 tbsp. Coconut Flour

Directions:

- Start by applying baking spray all over a microwave-safe mug.
- To this, stir in the protein powder, coconut flour, baking powder, and granulated sweetener. Mix well.
- Now, pour the cashew milk into the flour mixture along with vanilla extract. Tip: At this point, if the combination seems crumbly, add more milk to it until you get a thick batter.
- Next, cook in the microwave for 1 minute or until the center is set and cooked.

- Serve and enjoy.

Nutrition: Calories: 170; Fats: 6g; Carbohydrates: 7g; Protein: 29g

13 Apple Crumble

Preparation Time: 20 Minutes

Cooking Time: 25 Minutes

Servings: 6

Ingredients:

- 4 to 5 apples, cored and chopped (about 6 cups)
- ½ cup unsweetened applesauce, or ¼ cup water
- 2 to 3 tablespoons unrefined sugar (coconut, date, sucanat, maple syrup)
- 1 teaspoon ground cinnamon
- Pinch sea salt

Directions:

1. Preheat the oven to 350°F. Put the apples and applesauce in an 8-inch-square baking dish, and sprinkle with the sugar, cinnamon, and salt. Toss to combine.

2. In a medium bowl, mix together the nut butter and maple syrup until smooth and creamy. Add the oats, walnuts, cinnamon, and sugar and stir to coat using your hands if necessary. (If you have a small food processor, pulse the oats and walnuts together before adding them to the mix.)

3. Sprinkle the topping over the apples, and put the dish in the oven.

4. Bake for 20-25 minutes, or until the fruit is soft and the topping is lightly browned.

Nutrition: Calories: 356;   Fat: 17g; Carbohydrates: 49g; Protein: 7g

14 Cashew Chocolate Truffle

Preparation Time: 15 Minutes + 1 Hour to set

Cooking Time: 0 Minutes

Servings: 12

Ingredients:

- 1 cup raw cashews, soaked in water overnight
- ¾ cup pitted dates
- 2 tablespoons coconut oil
- 1 cup unsweetened shredded coconut, divided
- 1 to 2 tablespoons cocoa powder, to taste

Directions:

1. In a food processor, combine the cashews, dates, coconut oil, ½ cup of shredded coconut, and cocoa powder. Pulse until fully incorporated; it will resemble chunky cookie dough. Spread the remaining ½ cup of shredded coconut on a plate.
2. Form the mixture into tablespoon-size balls and roll on the plate to cover with the shredded coconut. Transfer to a parchment paper–lined plate or baking sheet. Repeat to make 12 truffles.
3. Place the truffles in the refrigerator for 1 hour to set. Transfer the truffles to a storage container or freezer-safe bag and seal.

Nutrition: Calories: 238; Protein: 3g; Carbohydrates: 16g; Fat: 18g

15 Banana Chocolate Cupcakes

Preparation Time: 20 Minutes

Cooking Time: 20 Minutes

Servings: 12

Ingredients:

- 3medium bananas
- 1 cup non-dairy milk
- 2 tablespoons almond butter
- 1 teaspoon apple cider vinegar
- 1 teaspoon pure vanilla extract
- 1¼ cups whole-wheat flour
- ½ cup rolled oats
- ¼ cup coconut sugar (optional)
- 1 teaspoon baking powder
- ½ teaspoon baking soda
- ½ cup unsweetened cocoa powder
- ¼ cup chia seeds, or sesame seeds
- Pinch sea salt
- ¼ cup dark chocolate chips, dried cranberries, or raisins (optional)

Directions:

1. Preheat the oven to 350°F. Lightly grease the cups of two 6-cup muffin tins or line with paper muffin cups.

2. Put the bananas, milk, almond butter, vinegar, and vanilla in a blender and purée until smooth, or stir together in a large bowl until smooth and creamy.

3. Put the flour, oats, sugar (if using), baking powder, baking soda, cocoa powder, chia seeds, salt, and chocolate chips in another large bowl, then stir to combine. Mix together the wet and dry ingredients, stirring as little as possible.

4. Spoon into muffin cups and bake for 20-25 minutes. Take the cupcakes out of the oven and let them cool fully before taking out of the muffin tins since they'll be very moist.

Nutrition: Calories: 215; Fat: 6g; Carbohydrates: 39g; Protein: 9g

16 Oranges with Cinnamon and Honey

Preparation Time: 5 Minutes

Cooking Time: 15 Minutes

Servings: 4

Ingredients:

- 10 1/2 ounces' orange
- 4 tablespoons honey
- 1 teaspoon cinnamon
- 1 ounce walnuts

Directions:

1. Peel the oranges, divide into slices.
2. Place the slices on a baking dish.
3. Chop the nuts.
4. Mix honey with cinnamon and nuts.
5. Sprinkle honey-nut mixture on oranges slices.
6. Preheat the oven to 390 °F. Then place the baking sheet in the oven and bake for 15 minutes.
5. You can eat orange slices cool or warm.

Nutrition: Calories: 179; Fat: 5g; Carbohydrates: 32g; Protein: 2g

17 Chocolate Fudge

Preparation Time: 10 Minutes

Cooking Time: 0 Minutes

Servings: 12

Ingredients:

- 4 oz unsweetened dark chocolate
- 3/4 cup coconut butter
- 15 drops liquid stevia
- 1 tsp vanilla extract

Directions:

1. Melt coconut butter and dark chocolate.
2. Add ingredients to the large bowl and combine well.
3. Pour mixture into a silicone loaf pan and place in refrigerator until set.
4. Cut into pieces and serve.

Nutrition: Calories: 157; Fat: 14g; Carbohydrates: 6g; Protein: 2g

18 Avocado Pudding

Preparation Time: 10 Minutes

Cooking Time: 0 minutes

Servings: 8

Ingredients:

- 2 ripe avocados, peeled, pitted and cut into pieces
- 1 tbsp fresh lime juice
- 14 oz can coconut milk
- 80 drops of liquid stevia
- 2 tsp vanilla extract

Directions:

1. Add all ingredients into the blender and blend until smooth.
2. Serve and enjoy.

Nutrition: Calories: 317; Fat: 30g; Protein: 3g; Carbohydrates: 9g

19 Oatmeal Sponge Cookies

Preparation Time: 10 Minutes

Cooking Time: 15 Minutes

Servings: 12

Ingredients:

- ¼ Cup Applesauce
- ½ Teaspoon Cinnamon
- 1/3 Cup Raisins
- ½ Teaspoon Vanilla Extract, Pure
- 1 cup Ripe Banana, Mashed
- 2 Cups Oatmeal

Directions:

1. Start by heating your oven to
2. Mix everything. It should be gooey.
3. Drop it onto an ungreased baking sheet by the tablespoon, and then flatten.
4. Bake for fifteen minutes.

Nutrition: Calories: 79; Total fat: 1g; Carbohydrates: 16g; Protein: 2g

20 Blueberry Mousse

Preparation Time: 20 Minutes

Cooking Time: 0 Minutes

Servings: 2

Ingredients:

- 1 cup wild blueberries
- 1 cup cashews, soaked for 10 minutes, drained
- 1/2 teaspoon berry powder
- 2 tablespoons coconut oil, melted
- 1 tablespoon lemon juice
- 1 teaspoon vanilla extract, unsweetened
- 1/4 cup hot water

Directions:

1. Mix all the ingredients in a food processor and process for 2 minutes until smooth.
2. Set aside until required.

Nutrition: Calories: 433; Total fat: 32g; Carbohydrates: 44g; Protein: 5g

21 Strawberry Mousse

Preparation Time: 5 Minutes

Cooking Time: 15 Minutes

Servings: 1

Ingredients:

- 8 ounces coconut milk, unsweetened
- 2 tablespoons honey
- 5 strawberries

Directions:

1. Place berries in a blender and pulse until the smooth mixture comes together.
2. Place milk in a bowl, whisk until whipped, and then add remaining ingredients and stir until combined.
3. Refrigerate the mousse for 10 minutes and then serve.

Nutrition: Calories: 145; Protein: 5g; Carbohydrates: 15g; Fats: 23g

22 Macha Coconut Cream Pie

Preparation Time: 15 Minutes + 4 Hours for freezing

Cooking Time: 0 Minutes

Servings: 4

Ingredients:

For the Crust:

- 1/2 cup ground flaxseed
- 3/4 cup shredded dried coconut
- 1 cup Medjool dates, pitted
- 3/4 cup dehydrated buckwheat groats
- 1/4 teaspoons sea salt

For the Filling:

- 1 cup dried coconut flakes
- 4 cups of coconut meat
- 1/4 cup and 2 Tablespoons coconut nectar
- 1/2 Tablespoons vanilla extract, unsweetened
- 1/4 teaspoons sea salt
- 2/3 cup and 2 Tablespoons coconut butter
- 1 tablespoon matcha powder
- 1/2 cup coconut water

Directions:

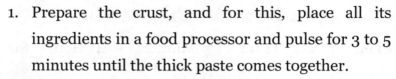

1. Prepare the crust, and for this, place all its ingredients in a food processor and pulse for 3 to 5 minutes until the thick paste comes together.
2. Take a 6-inch springform pan, grease it with oil, place crust mixture in it and spread and press the mixture evenly in the bottom and along the sides, and freeze until required.
3. Prepare the filling and place all its ingredients in a food processor and pulse for 2 minutes until it is smooth.
4. In the prepared pan, pour the filling into the smooth the top, and freeze for 4 hours until set.
5. Cut pie into slices and then serve.

Nutrition: Calories: 209; Fats: 18g; Carbohydrates: 10g; Protein: 1g

23 Peanut Butter Cheesecake

Preparation Time: 15 Minutes

Cooking Time: 20 Minutes

Servings: 8

Ingredients:

For the Crust:

- 1 cup dates, pitted, soaked in warm water for 10 minutes in water, drained
- 1/4 cup cocoa powder
- 3 Tablespoons melted coconut oil
- 1 cup rolled oats

For the Filling:

- 1 banana
- 1 1/2 cup cashews, soaked, drained
- 1/2 cup dates, pitted, soaked, drained
- 1/4 cup coconut oil
- 1 teaspoon vanilla extract, unsweetened
- 1/4 cup agave
- 1 cup peanut butter
- 1/2 cup coconut milk, chilled
- 1 tablespoon almond milk

For Garnish

- 2 tablespoons chocolate chips

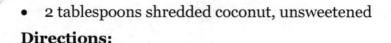

- 2 tablespoons shredded coconut, unsweetened

Directions:

1. Prepare the crust, and for this, place all its ingredients in a food processor and pulse for 3 to 5 minutes until the thick paste comes together.

2. Take a pie pan, grease it with oil, pour crust mixture in it and spread and press the mixture evenly in the bottom part and along the sides, and freeze until required.

3. Prepare the filling and place all its ingredients in a food processor and pulse for 2 minutes until it is smooth.

4. Pour the filling into the prepared pan, smooth the top, sprinkle chocolate chips and coconut on top and freeze for 4 hours until set.

5. Cut cake into slices and then serve.

Nutrition: Calories: 509; Fat: 32g; Carbs: 47g; Proteins: 11g

24 Orange Sorbet

Preparation Time: 4 Hours 5 Minutes

Cooking Time: 5 Minutes

Servings: 4

Ingredients:

- 2 ½ cups orange juice
- 2 stars anise
- ¾ cup coconut sugar, powdered

Directions:

1. Pour the juice into a medium saucepan, add star anise and sugar, and then place it over medium-high heat.
2. Bring the mixture to boil and keep stirring until sugar has dissolved, and then remove the star anise.
3. Remove pan from heat, let it cool completely, and then pour into a freezer-proof bowl.
4. Cover the bowl with its lid and then freeze for a minimum of 4 hours until firm, stirring every hour.
5. Serve when ready.

Nutrition: Calories: 88; Protein: 0g; Carbohydrates: 22g; Fat: 0g

25 Baked Apples

Preparation Time: 5 Minutes

Cooking Time: 30 Minutes

Servings: 4

Ingredients:

- 6 apples, medium, peeled, cut into chunks
- 2 tablespoon coconut oil
- 1 teaspoon ground cinnamon

Directions:

1. Switch on the oven, then set it to 350 degrees F (177 °C) and let it preheat.
2. Meanwhile, place oil in a small bowl and then stir in cinnamon until combined.
3. Arrange apple pieces in a medium baking dish, drizzle cinnamon mixture over them, toss until coated, and then bake for 30 minutes until softened, stirring halfway.
4. Serve straight away.

Nutrition: Calories: 170; Fat: 4g; Carbohydrates: 31g; Protein: 5g

26 Raspberry Cream Pie

Preparation Time: 10 Minutes + 3 Hours for chilling

Cooking Time: 0 Minutes

Servings: 10

Ingredients:

Crust:

- 2 cups almonds
- 2 cups dates
- A pinch of sea salt
- A pinch of ground cloves
- 1/4 teaspoon ground anise
- 2 tablespoons coconut oil, softened

Filling:

- 2 ripe bananas
- 2 frozen bananas
- 2 cups raspberries
- 1 tablespoon agave syrup
- 2 tablespoons coconut oil, softened

Directions:

1. In your food processor, blend the crust ingredients until the mixture comes together; press the crust into a lightly oiled springform pan.

2. Then, blend the filling layer. Spoon the filling onto the crust, creating a flat surface with a spatula.

3. Transfer the cake to your freezer for about 3 hours. Store in your freezer.
4. Bon appétit!

Nutrition: Calories: 225; Fat: 6g; Carbohydrates: 49g; Protein: 2g

27 Tropical Bread Pudding

Preparation Time: 60 Minutes

Cooking Time: 60 Minutes

Servings: 5

Ingredients:

- 6 cups stale bread, cut into cubes
- 2 cups rice milk, sweetened
- 1/2 cup agave syrup
- 1 teaspoon vanilla extract
- 1/2 teaspoon ground cloves
- 1 teaspoon ground cinnamon
- 1/4 teaspoon coarse sea salt
- 5 tablespoons pineapple, crushed and drained
- 1 firm banana, sliced

Directions:

1. Place the bread cubes in a lightly oiled baking dish.
2. Now, blend the milk, agave syrup, vanilla, ground cloves, cinnamon and coarse sea salt until creamy and uniform.
3. Fold in the pineapple and banana and mix to combine well.
4. Spoon the mixture all over the bread cubes; press down slightly and set aside for about 1 hour.

5. Bake in the preheated oven at 350 degrees F for about 1 hour or until the top of your pudding is golden brown. Bon appétit!

Nutrition: Calories: 443; Fat: 5g; Carbohydrates: 96g; Protein: 8g

28 Apricot and Pecan Crum Pie

Preparation Time: 15 Minutes

Cooking Time: 45 Minutes

Servings: 9

Ingredients:

- 1 pound apricots, pitted and halved
- 1 tablespoon fresh lemon juice
- 1 tablespoon crystallized ginger
- 1 cup brown sugar
- 1/2 cup rolled oats
- 1 cup all-purpose flour
- 1 teaspoon baking powder
- 1/2 teaspoon baking soda
- 1/2 teaspoon ground cloves
- 1/2 teaspoon ground anise
- 1/2 teaspoon ground cinnamon
- 1 teaspoon vanilla essence
- 1/4 teaspoon kosher salt
- 1/2 cup coconut oil, softened
- 1/3 cup pecans, roughly chopped

Directions:

1. Start by preheating your oven to 350 degrees F.

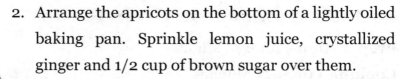

2. Arrange the apricots on the bottom of a lightly oiled baking pan. Sprinkle lemon juice, crystallized ginger and 1/2 cup of brown sugar over them.

3. In a mixing bowl, thoroughly combine the oats, all-purpose flour, baking powder, baking soda, 1/2 cup of brown sugar, ground cloves, anise, cinnamon, vanilla, salt and coconut oil.

4. Fold in the pecans and stir to combine. Spread the topping mixture over the apricot layer.

5. Bake in the preheated oven for about 45 minutes or until golden brown. Bon appétit.

Nutrition: Calories: 322; Fat: 15g; Protein: 3g; Carbohydrates: 49g

29 Apricot Dump Cake

Preparation Time: 10 Minutes

Cooking Time: 40 minutes

Servings: 6

Ingredients:

- 10 apricots, pitted and halved
- 1 tablespoon crystallized ginger
- 1/4 cup brown sugar
- 1 cup all-purpose flour
- 1 teaspoon baking powder
- 1/2 teaspoon ground cinnamon
- 4 tablespoons agave syrup
- A pinch of kosher salt
- A pinch of grated nutmeg
- 1/4 cup coconut oil, room temperature
- 1/2 cup almond milk

Directions:

1. Arrange the apricots on the bottom of a lightly oiled baking pan. Sprinkle ginger and brown sugar over them.

2. In a mixing bowl, thoroughly combine the flour, baking powder, cinnamon, agave syrup, salt and nutmeg.

3. Add in the coconut oil and almond milk and mix until everything is well incorporated. Spread the topping mixture over the fruit layer.
4. Bake your cake at 360 degrees F for about 40 minutes or until the top is golden brown. Bon appétit!

Nutrition: Calories: 226; Total fat: 7g; Carbohydrates: 39; Protein: 2g

30 Sweet Potato Spice Cake

Preparation Time: 5 Minutes

Cooking Time: 45 Minutes

Servings: 6

Ingredients:

- 1 sweet potato, cooked and peeled
- ½ cup unsweetened applesauce
- ½ cup plant-based milk
- ¼ cup maple syrup
- 1 teaspoon vanilla extract
- 2 cups whole-wheat flour
- ½ teaspoon baking soda
- ½ teaspoon ground cinnamon
- ¼ teaspoon ground ginger

Directions:

1 Preheat the oven to 350°F.

2 In a large mixing bowl, use a fork or potato masher to mash the sweet potato.

3 Mix in the applesauce, milk, maple syrup, and vanilla.

4 Stir in the flour, baking soda, cinnamon, and ginger until the dry ingredients have been thoroughly combined with the wet ingredients.

5 Pour the batter into a nonstick baking dish or one lined with parchment paper. Bake for 45 minutes, or until you can stick a knife into the middle of the cake and it comes out clean.

6 Cool, slice, and serve.

Nutrition: Calories: 238; Total fat: 1g; Carbohydrates: 52g; Protein: 5g

31 Chocolate Microwave Mug Cake

Preparation Time: 5 Minutes + 5 Minutes to cool

Cooking Time: 90 Seconds Minutes

Servings: 1

Ingredients:

- 3 tablespoons whole-wheat flour
- 3 tablespoons unsweetened applesauce
- 1 tablespoon cocoa powder
- 1 tablespoon maple syrup
- 1 tablespoon plant-based milk
- 1 teaspoon vanilla extract
- ¼ teaspoon baking powder

Directions:

1. In a microwave-safe coffee mug or bowl, combine the flour, applesauce, cocoa powder, maple syrup, milk, vanilla, and baking powder. Stir together until there are no clumps of dry flour left. (Place the mug on a paper towel or plate to ensure easy cleanup.)

1. Microwave on high for 90 seconds, or until the cake has risen to the top of the mug.

2. Remove from the microwave and set aside to cool for a minimum of 5 minutes before serving.

Nutrition: Calories: 185; Protein: 4g; Carbohydrates: 41g; Fats: 3g

32 Oat Crunch Apple Crisp

Preparation Time: 10 Minutes

Cooking Time: 35 Minutes

Servings: 6

Ingredients:

- 3 medium apples, cored and cut into ¼-inch pieces
- ¾ cup apple juice
- 1 teaspoon vanilla extract
- 1 teaspoon ground cinnamon, divided
- 2 cups rolled oats
- ¼ cup maple syrup

Directions:

1. Preheat the oven to 375°F.
2. In a large bowl, combine the apple slices, apple juice, vanilla, and ½ teaspoon of cinnamon. Mix well to thoroughly coat the apple slices.
3. Layer the apple slices on the bottom of a round or square baking dish. Take any leftover liquid and pour it over the apple slices.
4. In a large bowl, stir together the oats, maple syrup, and the remaining ½ teaspoon of cinnamon until the oats are completely coated.

5. Sprinkle the oat mixture over the apples, being sure to spread it out evenly so that none of the apple slices are visible.

6. Bake for 35 minutes, or until the oats begin to turn golden brown, and serve.

Nutrition: Calories: 213; Fats: 2g; Carbohydrates: 47g; Protein: 4g

33 Cherry Nice Cream

Preparation Time: 10 Minutes

Cooking Time: 0 Minutes

Servings: 6

Ingredients:

- 6 frozen bananas, peeled, cut into chunks
- 3 cups frozen pitted cherries

Directions:

1 In a food processor, combine the bananas and cherries and purée, scraping down the sides of the blender jar as needed, until smooth and creamy.

2 Serve immediately.

Nutrition: Calories: 154; Fat: 1g; Carbohydrates: 39g; Protein: 2g

34 Date Truffle

Preparation Time: 10 Minutes + 1 Hour chilling

Cooking Time: 0 Minutes

Servings: 12

Ingredients:

- 1 cup raw cashews
- 2 cups boiling water
- ¾ cup pitted dates
- ¼ cup gluten-free rolled oats
- 1 cup unsweetened shredded coconut
- 2 tablespoons unsweetened cocoa powder

Directions:

1 Line a baking sheet with parchment paper.

2 In a small bowl, combine the cashews and boiling water and let sit for 30 minutes. Drain the cashews, reserving the soaking water.

3 In a food processor, combine the cashews, dates, oats, coconut, and cocoa powder and pulse until fully combined, adding the reserved cashew soaking water 1 tablespoon at a time as needed to achieve a chunky cookie dough–like texture.

4 Scoop 1 tablespoon of the mixture, form it into a ball, and set it on the prepared baking sheet. Repeat with the remaining mixture.

5 Refrigerate for 1 hour before serving. The truffles can be stored in an airtight container in the refrigerator for up to 5 days.

Nutrition: Calories: 127; Protein: 3g; Carbohydrates: 13g; Fat: 8g

35 Cashew No Bake Cookies

Preparation Time: 15 Minutes + 1 Hour chilling

Cooking Time: 5 Minutes

Servings: 8

Ingredients:

- 2 tablespoons pure maple syrup
- 2 tablespoons unsweetened plant-based milk
- ⅔ cup natural cashew butter or another nut butter
- 1 cup quinoa flakes
- ¼ cup finely chopped raw cashews (optional)

Directions:

1. Line a baking sheet with parchment paper.
2. In a saucepan, combine the maple syrup and plant-based milk and cook over medium-high heat until it just begins to bubble.
3. Remove the pan from the heat, add the cashew butter, and stir until well combined. Add the quinoa flakes and chopped cashews (if using) and mix well.
4. Using a cookie scoop or tablespoon, scoop out 2 tablespoons of the mixture and place it on the prepared baking sheet. Repeat with the remaining mixture.

5. Refrigerate for at least 1 hour before serving. The cookies can be stored in an airtight container in the refrigerator for up to 5 days.

Nutrition: Calories: 189; Fat: 11g; Carbohydrates: 18g; Protein: 6g

36 Vanilla Cupcakes

Preparation Time: 5 Minutes
Cooking Time: 20 Minutes
Servings: 12
Ingredients:

- 1 teaspoon baking powder
- 1½ cups unbleached all-purpose flour
- ½ teaspoon sea salt (optional)
- ½ cup organic virgin coconut oil, at room temperature (optional)
- ¾ cup pure maple syrup, at room temperature (optional)
- 1 teaspoon pure vanilla extract
- ¾ cup unsweetened almond milk, at room temperature

Directions:

1. Preheat the oven to 350°F (180°C). Line a muffin pan with 12 paper liners.
2. Mix the baking powder, flour, and salt (if desired) in a medium mixing bowl.
3. Beat the oil (if desired) and maple syrup (if desired) in the bowl of a stand mixer fitted with a paddle attachment (or use a whisk if you don't have a mixer). Stir in the vanilla.

4. Starting and ending with the dry ingredients, and add $^1/_3$ of the flour mixture to the oil mixture alternately with the almond milk. Stir to combine, scraping down the sides of the bowl as needed.

5. Scrape the batter into the prepared muffin cups, filling each about three-quarters full.

6. Bake in the preheated oven for 15 to 20 minutes, or until the tops are golden and a toothpick inserted in the middle comes out clean.

7. Allow the muffins to cool for 10 minutes in the muffin pan before removing and serving.

Nutrition: Calories: 193; Fat: 9g; Carbohydrates: 28g; Protein: 0.6g

37 Maple Raisin Oatmeal Cookies

Preparation Time: 15 Minutes

Cooking Time: 10 minutes

Servings: 36

Ingredients:

- 1 cup whole wheat flour
- 1 teaspoon ground cinnamon
- ½ teaspoon baking soda
- ½ teaspoon sea salt (optional)
- ½ teaspoon baking powder
- ¼ teaspoon ground nutmeg
- ½ cup pure maple syrup (optional)
- ½ cup organic virgin coconut oil, at room temperature (optional)
- 1 /3 cup almond butter
- 1 teaspoon pure vanilla extract
- 1 vegan egg
- 1½ cups gluten-free rolled oats
- ¾ cup raisins

Directions:

1. Mix the flour, cinnamon, baking soda, salt (if desired), baking powder, and nutmeg in a medium mixing bowl.

2. In a stand mixer fitted with the paddle attachment, beat together the maple syrup (if desired), oil (if desired), almond butter, vanilla, egg, and egg yolk. Add the flour mixture, a little at a time, mixing after each addition until just incorporated. You'll need to scrape down the sides as needed. Fold in the oats and raisins and mix again. Place the dough in a refrigerator until firmed and chilled.

3. Preheat the oven to 350°F (180°C). Line 2 baking sheets with parchment paper.

4. Using a spoon or mini ice cream scoop, drop about 2 tablespoons of the dough onto the parchment-lined baking sheets for each cookie, spacing them 2 inches apart. Flatten each a bit with the back of a spoon.

5. Bake for 10 to 12 minutes, or until the cookies are golden brown.

6. Transfer the baking sheets onto a wire rack to cool completely before serving.

Nutrition: Calories: 257; Fat: 14g; Carbohydrates: 33g; Protein: 6g

38 Vanilla Frosting

Preparation Time: 10 Minutes

Cooking Time: 0 minutes

Servings: 1 ½ cup

Ingredients:

- 1 teaspoon vanilla extract (or seeds from 1 vanilla bean)
- 3 ounces raw, unsalted cashews (about ¾ cup)
- 5 ounces pitted dates (8 to 9 Medjool or 16 to 18 Deglet Noor), chopped
- ¾ cup water, plus more as needed

Directions:

1. In a blender, add the vanilla, cashews, dates, and ¾ cup water. If the cashews and dates aren't covered completely, add more water as needed. Let sit for at least 45 minutes, or until the nuts and dates are thoroughly softened.
2. Blitz until the mixture is smooth and creamy. You'll need to stop the blender occasionally to scrape down the sides. Add a little more water if a thinner consistency is desired.
3. Serve chilled.

Nutrition: Calories: 875; Fat: 37g; Protein: 18g; Carbohydrates: 32g

39 Mint Chocolate Chip Sorbet

Preparation Time: 5 Minutes

Cooking Time: 0 Minutes

Servings: 3

Ingredients:

- 1 frozen banana
- 1 tablespoon almond butter, or peanut butter, or other nut or seed butter
- 2 tablespoons fresh mint, minced
- ¼ cup or less non-dairy milk (only if needed)
- 2 to 3 tablespoons non-dairy chocolate chips, or cocoa nibs
- 2 to 3 tablespoons goji berries (optional)

Directions:

1. Put the banana, almond butter, and mint in a food processor or blender and purée until smooth.
2. Add the non-dairy milk if needed to keep blending (but only if needed, as this will make the texture less solid). Pulse the chocolate chips and goji berries (if using) into the mix so they're roughly chopped up.

Nutrition: Calories: 212; Total fat: 10g; Carbohydrates: 31g; Protein: 3g

40 Ginger Spice Brownies

Preparation Time: 5 Minutes

Cooking Time: 35 Minutes

Servings: 612

Ingredients:

- 1¾ cups whole-grain flour
- 1 teaspoon baking powder
- 1 teaspoon baking soda
- ½ teaspoon salt
- 1 tablespoon ground ginger
- ½ teaspoon ground cinnamon
- ½ teaspoon ground allspice
- 3 tablespoons unsweetened cocoa powder
- ½ cup vegan semisweet chocolate chips
- ½ cup chopped walnuts
- ¼ cup canola oil
- ½ cup dark molasses
- ½ cup water
- ⅓ cup light brown sugar
- 2 teaspoons grated fresh ginger

Directions:

1   Preheat the oven to 350°F. Grease an 8-inch square baking pan and set aside. In a large bowl, combine

the flour, baking powder, baking soda, salt, ground ginger, cinnamon, allspice, and cocoa. Stir in the chocolate chips and walnuts and set aside.

2   In medium bowl, combine the oil, molasses, water, sugar, and fresh ginger, then mix well.

3   Pour the wet ingredients into the dry ingredients and mix well.

4   Scrape the dough into the prepared baking pan. The dough will be sticky, so wet your hands to press it evenly into the pan.

5   Bake until a toothpick inserted in the center comes out clean, for 30-35 minutes. Cool on a wire rack 30 minutes before cutting. Store in an airtight container.

Nutrition: Calories: 422; Total fat: 21g; Carbohydrates: 58g; Protein: 4g

41 Cherry Vanilla Rice Pudding (pressure cooker)

Preparation Time: 5 Minutes
Cooking Time: 30 Minutes
Servings: 6
Ingredients:

- 1 cup short-grain brown rice
- 1¾ cups nondairy milk, plus more as needed
- 1½ cups water
- 4 tablespoons unrefined sugar or pure maple syrup (use 2 tablespoons if you use a sweetened milk), plus more as needed
- 1 teaspoon vanilla extract (use ½ teaspoon if you use vanilla milk)
- Pinch salt
- ¼ cup dried cherries or ½ cup fresh or frozen pitted cherries

Directions:

1. In your electric pressure cooker's cooking pot, combine the rice, milk, water, sugar, vanilla, and salt.
2. High pressure for 30 minutes

3. Close and lock the lid and ensure the pressure valve is sealed, then select High Pressure and set the time for 30 minutes.

4. Once the cook time is complete, let the pressure release naturally, about 20 minutes. Once all the pressure has released, carefully unlock and remove the lid. Stir in the cherries and put the lid back on loosely for about 10 minutes. Serve, adding more milk or sugar, as desired.

Nutrition: Calories: 177; Protein: 3g; Carbohydrates: 52g; Fats: 1g

42 Mango Coconut Cream Pie

Preparation Time: 20 Minutes + 30 Minutes Chilling

Cooking Time: 0 Minutes

Servings: 8

Ingredients:

Crust

- ½ cup rolled oats
- 1 cup cashews
- 1 cup soft pitted dates

Filling

- 1 cup canned coconut milk
- ½ cup water
- 2 large mangos, peeled and chopped, or about 2 cups frozen chunks
- ½ cup unsweetened shredded coconut

Directions:

1. Put all the crust ingredients in a food processor and pulse until it holds together. If you don't have a food processor, chop everything as finely as possible and use ½ cup cashew or almond butter in place of half the cashews. Press the mixture down firmly into an 8-inch pie or springform pan.

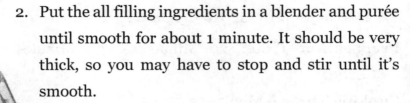

2. Put the all filling ingredients in a blender and purée until smooth for about 1 minute. It should be very thick, so you may have to stop and stir until it's smooth.

3. Pour the filling into the crust, use a rubber spatula to smooth the top, and put the pie in the freezer until set. Once frozen, it should be set out for about 15 minutes to soften before serving.

4. Top with a batch of Coconut Whipped Cream scooped on top of the pie once it's set. Finish it off with a sprinkling of toasted shredded coconut.

Nutrition: Calories: 427; Fats: 28g; Carbohydrates: 45g; Protein: 8g

43 Peanut Butter Cookies

Preparation Time: 5 Minutes
Cooking Time: 10 Minutes
Servings: 12
Ingredients:

- 1 cup natural peanut butter
- ¼ cup maple syrup
- 1 teaspoon vanilla extract
- 1 teaspoon salt

Directions:

1. Preheat the oven to 350°F. Line a baking sheet with parchment paper.
2. In a large bowl, mix together the peanut butter, maple syrup, vanilla extract, and salt until well blended.
3. Scoop generous tablespoon portions of the dough onto the prepared sheet pan. With a fork, press the cookies down slightly and make crosswise indentations in the cookies.
4. Bake in the oven for 8 minutes, until the cookies begin to turn golden. Remove from the oven and let sit on the baking sheet for 10 minutes. Gently transfer the cookies to a wire rack and let cool completely.

Nutrition: Calories: 156; Fat: 11g; Carbohydrates: 10g; Protein: 7g

44 Chocolate Mug Cake

Preparation Time: 5 Minutes

Cooking Time: 10 Minutes

Servings: 2

Ingredients:

- Oil or nonstick cooking spray, for greasing the mugs
- 6 tablespoons all-purpose flour
- 3 tablespoons sugar
- 2½ tablespoons unsweetened cocoa powder
- ½ teaspoon baking powder
- ¼ cup vegan dark chocolate chips
- 2 tablespoons vegetable oil
- 6 tablespoons almond milk
- 1 teaspoon vanilla extract

Directions:

1. Preheat the oven to 350°F, and lightly grease two large oven-safe mugs with oil or cooking spray.
2. In a medium bowl, combine the flour, sugar, cocoa powder, baking powder, chocolate chips, vegetable oil, almond milk, and vanilla extract. Stir well to combine.
3. Pour the mixture evenly into the mugs, and bake in the oven for 15 minutes, until a cake tester or toothpick inserted into the middle comes out clean.

4. Transfer the mugs to a wire rack and let cool for 10 minutes. Turn out onto plates or enjoy right from the mug.

Nutrition: Calories: 425; Protein: 6g; Carbohydrates: 57g; Fat: 22g

45 Avocado and Pumpkin Brownies with Dried Fruit

Preparation Time: 5 Minutes
Cooking Time: 20 Minutes
Servings: 12
Ingredients:

- 1 ripe avocado, peeled and pitted
- ½ cup unsweetened pumpkin purée
- ½ cup natural peanut butter
- 2 tablespoons maple syrup
- ¼ cup plus 3 tablespoons coconut milk
- 3 tablespoons unsweetened cocoa powder
- 1 teaspoon vanilla extract
- ¼ cup dried chopped fruit such as cherries or apricots
- ½ cup dark chocolate chips (regular or vegan)

Directions:

1. Preheat the oven to 375°F. Line a standard 9-inch loaf pan with parchment paper and set aside.
2. In a blender or food processor, blend together the avocado, pumpkin purée, peanut butter, maple syrup, coconut milk, cocoa powder, and vanilla

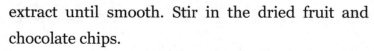

extract until smooth. Stir in the dried fruit and chocolate chips.

3. Transfer the mixture to the prepared pan, spreading evenly.

4. Bake for 20 minutes, until a cake tester or toothpick comes out clean.

5. Let the pan cool on a metal rack for a few minutes and then cut into 1½-inch pieces. Refrigerate.

Nutrition: Calories: 190; Fat: 11g; Carbohydrates: 21g; Protein: 5g

46 Last Minute Macaroons

Preparation Time: 4 Minutes

Cooking Time: 10 Minutes

Servings: 10

Ingredients:

- 3 cups coconut flakes, sweetened
- 9 ounces canned coconut milk, sweetened
- 1 teaspoon ground anise
- 1 teaspoon vanilla extract

Directions:

1. Set the oven to 325 degrees F. Line the cookie sheets with parchment paper.
2. Thoroughly combine all the ingredients until everything is well incorporated.
3. Using a cookie scoop, drop mounds of the batter onto the prepared cookie sheets.
4. Bake for at least 11 minutes until they are lightly browned. Bon appétit!

Nutrition: Calories: 125; Fat: 7g; Carbohydrates: 14g; Protein: 1g

47 Raw Walnut and Berry Cake

Preparation Time: 10 Minutes + 3 Hours chilling

Cooking Time: 0 Minutes

Servings: 8

Ingredients:

- 1 ½ cups walnuts, ground
- 2 tablespoons maple syrup
- 1/4 cup raw cacao powder
- 1/4 teaspoon ground cinnamon
- A pinch of coarse salt
- A pinch of freshly grated nutmeg
- Berry layer:
- 6 cups mixed berries
- 2 frozen bananas
- 1/2 cup agave syrup

Directions:

1. In your food processor, blend the crust ingredients until the mixture comes together; press the crust into a lightly oiled baking pan.
2. Then, blend the berry layer. Spoon the berry layer onto the crust, creating a flat surface with a spatula.
3. Transfer the cake to your freezer for about 3 hours. Store in your freezer. Bon appétit!

Nutrition: Calories: 244; Fat: 10g; Carbohydrates: 39g; Protein: 4g

48 Mini Lemon Tarts

Preparation Time: 15 Minutes + freezing time

Cooking Time: 0 Minutes

Servings: 9

Ingredients:

- 1 cup cashews
- 1 cup dates, pitted
- 1/2 cup coconut flakes
- 1/2 teaspoon anise, ground
- 3 lemons, freshly squeezed
- 1 cup coconut cream
- 2 tablespoons agave syrup

Directions:

1. Brush a muffin tin with nonstick cooking oil.
2. Blend the cashews, dates, coconut, and anise in your food processor or a high-speed blender. Press the crust into the peppered muffin tin.
3. Then, blend the lemon, coconut cream, and agave syrup. Spoon the cream into the muffin tin.
4. Store in your freezer. Bon appétit!

Nutrition: Calories: 257; Fat: 16g; Protein: 4g; Carbohydrates: 25g

49 Raspberries Cheesecake

Preparation Time: 15 Minutes + 3 Hours freezing
Cooking Time: 0 Minutes
Servings: 9
Ingredients:

Crust:

- 2 cups almonds
- 1 cup fresh dates, pitted
- 1/4 teaspoon ground cinnamon

Filling:

- 2 cups raw cashews, soaked overnight
- 14 ounces blackberries, frozen
- 1 tablespoon fresh lime juice
- 1/4 teaspoon crystallized ginger
- 1 can coconut cream
- 8 fresh dates, pitted

Directions:

1. In your food processor, blend the crust ingredients until the mixture comes together; press the crust into a lightly oiled spring form pan.
2. Then, blend the filling layer until completely smooth. Spoon the filling onto the crust, creating a flat surface with a spatula.

3. Transfer the cake to your freezer for about 3 hours. Store in your freezer.

4. Garnish with organic citrus peel. Bon appétit!

   Nutrition: Calories: 385; Fat: 23g; Carbohydrates: 41g; Protein: 11g

50 Chocolate Mango Pie

Preparation Time: 10 Minutes + 3 Hours freezing

Cooking Time: 0 Minutes

Servings: 16

Ingredients:

Avocado layer:

- 3 ripe avocados, pitted and peeled
- A pinch of sea salt
- A pinch of ground anise
- 1/2 teaspoon vanilla paste
- 2 tablespoons coconut milk
- 5 tablespoons agave syrup
- 1/3 cup cocoa powder

Crema layer:

- 1/3 cup almond butter
- 1/2 cup coconut cream
- 1 medium mango, peeled
- 1/2 coconut flakes
- 2 tablespoons agave syrup

Directions:

1. In your food processor, blend the avocado layer until smooth and uniform; reserve.

2. Then, blend the other layer in a separate bowl. Spoon the layers in a lightly oiled baking pan.

3. Transfer the cake to your freezer for about 3 hours. Store in your freezer. Bon appétit!

Nutrition: Calories: 196; Fat: 17g; Carbohydrates: 14g; Protein: 2g

Conclusion

Eating more plant nourishments is related with life span and diminished hazard for most incessant infections, including coronary illness and type 2 diabetes. Plant nourishments, (for example, entire grains, beans, organic products, vegetables, nuts, and seeds) are plentiful in wellbeing advancing supplements and mixes like nutrients, minerals, fiber, and phytochemicals. Yet, plants can likewise be a decent wellspring of protein.

What is Protein? Proteins are found in the cells and tissues of every single living thing. They are chains of amino acids, particles that are associated with an assortment of natural capacities. There are 20 amino acids, nine of which can't be incorporated in the human body and should be obtained through diet. These are known as basic amino acids. Most plant nourishments are considered "fragmented" proteins, because they ordinarily have low degrees of, or are missing, at least one of the fundamental amino acids.

For instance, grains are low in the amino corrosive lysine, however have satisfactory methionine. Vegetables (beans, lentils, chickpeas, peas, and peanuts), then again, contain sufficient lysine, however are low in methionine. In this manner, a dietary example that incorporates both entire grains and vegetables will give an adequate measure of all basic amino acids. In spite of the fact that it was once felt that integral nourishments like these should have been devoured simultaneously, it is currently comprehended that eating an assortment of plant food sources for the duration of the day can give all the amino acids the body needs.

Most Americans get a lot of protein in their diets. "Generally, given the nourishments normally accessible, protein admission is certainly not a significant worry in the U.S., regardless of whether somebody follows a plant-based diet," says Alice H. Lichtenstein, DSc, chief of Tufts' HNRCA Cardiovascular Nutrition Laboratory and official editorial manager of Tufts Health and Nutrition Letter.

A Plant-Based Diet: Typical plant-based diets are veggie lover (which incorporates dairy items and eggs alongside plant nourishments) and vegan (which wipes out every single creature item, including nectar), yet a "plant-based" diet can likewise be one that basically boosts plant nourishment consumption and lessens creature proteins.

Not all plant-based dietary examples are similarly helpful. Analysts from Tufts University as of late distributed an examination in The Journal of Nutrition which found that plant-based dietary examples with significant levels of insignificantly handled plant nourishments (like entire grains, beans, nuts/seeds, organic products, and vegetables) were related with lower danger of all-cause mortality, yet plant-based diets with low degrees of these decisions were most certainly not. "The key is to ensure you follow a 'sound' plant-based diet wealthy in negligibly handled nourishments, not one dependent on refined grains and profoundly prepared lousy nourishment," says Lichtenstein.

Research, remembering a recent report by Nielsen and associates for the diary Nutrients, has indicated that dinners dependent on plant protein sources like beans are similarly as filling and fulfilling as suppers containing creature proteins. For a totally plant-based diet, eating a wide assortment of plant nourishments guarantees that fundamental amino corrosive prerequisites are met.

As indicated by a 2018 report by a worldwide data organization, buyer interest for plant-based protein is

developing. Fourteen percent of U.S. purchasers reviewed for the report demonstrated normally devouring plant-based protein sources, for example, tofu and veggie burgers, despite the fact that most by far didn't think about themselves vegan or veggie lover. Picking plant-based proteins has a dietary effect past protein quality. "We don't eat a nourishment or gathering of nourishments just to get a solitary supplement (like protein)," says Lichtenstein. "Supplanting creature proteins with plant nourishments like beans, for instance, expands admission of fiber, which is commonly under-expended in the American diet."

Other than potential medical advantages, going meatless only one day seven days can possibly lessen ozone harming substance discharges and add to the general soundness of the planet.

CPSIA information can be obtained
at www.ICGtesting.com
Printed in the USA
BVHW090534170421
605144BV00002B/256